Summary and ~~Analysis~~

of

12 Rules for Life:

An Antidote to Chaos

by

Jordan B. Peterson

BOOK TIGERS

9 781471 703676

Note to Readers:

This is an unofficial Summary & Analysis of 12 Rules for Life: An Antidote to Chaos by Jordan B. Peterson, designed to enrich your reading experience.

Scan here to buy the original book.

not sponsor or endorse our publications. This book is unofficial and unauthorized. It is not authorized, approved, licensed, or endorsed by the aforementioned interests or any of their licensees.

The information in this book has been provided for educational and entertainment purposes only.

The information contained in this book has been compiled from sources deemed reliable and it is accurate to the best of the Author's knowledge; however, the Author cannot guarantee its accuracy and validity and cannot be held liable for any errors or omissions. Upon using the information contained in this book, you agree to hold harmless the author from and against any damages, costs, and expenses, including any legal fees, potentially resulting from the application of any of the information provided by this guide. The disclaimer applies to any damages or injury caused by the use and application, whether directly or indirectly, of any advice or information presented, whether for breach of contract, tort, neglect, personal injury, criminal intent, or under any other cause of action. You agree to accept all risks of using the information presented inside this book.

The fact that an individual or organization is referred to in this document as a citation or source of information does not imply that the author or publisher endorses the information that the individual or organization provided. This is an unofficial summary & analytical review and has not been approved by the original author of the book.

Download Your Free Gift

Before you go any further, why not pick up a gift from us to you?

Investing In You – Using the Power of Positive Thinking.

You will understand the true power of your positive thinking and subconscious mind and you will have absolute control over them, very fast!

Scan the QR code to get it before it expires!

Table of Contents

Summary Overview

1
2 Rules for Life: An Antidote to Chaos is not a simple list of rules or an explanation of each rule. It is a book of stories, theories, and a new way to look at life. Author Jordan Peterson has not had a perfect life, but no one has a perfect life. Life is full of suffering and pain, but we cease to exist without this suffering and inequality. Without inequality, nothing has value. This is not exactly a self-help book, nor is it a simple rule book, but about understanding life's dichotomy. We must learn to find balance, the good, bad, fair, unfair, differences, and similarities. The book itself is broken into 12 rules, designed, and separated as chapters. The stories are relatable and applicable, not just to the rules, but to life. The detailed read helps us understand ourselves as beings, part of the human race that collectively suffers but also finds joy.

The opening is a summary of why this book was written. It ironically started with the author writing answers to questions on a website where other anonymous uses chose whether to raise or lower the answer based on their feelings. Few responses ever really get a high number, and the author largely had the same experience. That is until he answered a question about the 12 things in life that can bring happiness or that you should always do. Some of these were straight and serious, others were very tongue in cheek type writing, but the list was the height of popularity on that platform. The list served as the basis for the chapters of this book. Perhaps this is because people like lists, but the order can become obsessive if we are not careful.

On the other hand, chaos can overwhelm and drown us if we do not have some order. We must stay on the straight path, and this book is a guide for doing so with 12 "rules." This will help us to live properly, in a sustainable way.

Rule 1

The first rule, each rule corresponding to a chapter, is "Stand Up Straight with Your Shoulders Back." As with the other rules, a story is included to help with the understanding of each. This one is based on lobsters and territory. Most people do not spend a lot of time thinking about lobsters unless it is a meal, but lobsters have helped scientists map and understand the brain and neural circuit for a long time. Lobsters had a somewhat simple nervous system with neurons that are easy to observe and map. By mapping the lobster's neural pathways that of more complex animals and humans can also be understood.

Lobsters are much like humans in the sense that they want a home or a secure base from which they can hunt, scavenge; this home base allows them to eat from whatever chaos and prey may rain down from above. This creates a problem, though. Two lobsters or multiple lobsters and young may want to live in the same area, feeding off the same things that fall to their home. Other animals, like birds, do the same. To humans, birds singing can sound beautiful, but for the birds, it is a warning system that others should stay away because this is their home turf and place to be considered home. Take the wren, for example. This small bird is actually ruthless and highly territorial. A story of two birdhouses is shared in which one was built with a small opening that only a tiny bird, like a wren, would fit in, which it quickly did. The neighbor had a larger birdhouse with an opening for a bigger bird, like a robin. However, when the wren took up residence in the smaller ones, it filled the larger house with sticks so no other large bird could move in. The removal of the sticks would have just caused the wren to repeat the work. This tiny bird was protecting what it considered its territory. Both lobsters and wrens are obsessed with position and status, though in very different worlds.

Since territory matters and the best of locales are in short supply, conflict is created. This conflict leads to the issue of trying to win or lose without incurring great costs. Since neither side wants to lose too much, animals that have to cohabitate in the same area have learned tricks to show dominance at little cost. For example, a defeated wolf will turn over and show its throat, but the dominant will rarely tear into the throat because a future hunting partner may be needed. If the territory wars do continue, both wolves, lobsters, and even birds are at risk of getting hurt, making them easy prey later on. Losing this type of battle, especially one in which some type of physical or mental injury is sustained, causes the brain to change, and the creature becomes a bottom dog or low man on the totem pole, so to speak. They will be less likely to try again in the future. The brain chemistry changes and more serotonin means the lobster will likely be more cocky, self-assured, and fight longer. The same principle applies to humans who take selective serotonin reuptake inhibitors, SSRIs.

When a lobster who loses a fight does fight again, they are more likely to lose again. The opposite is true for winners who are more likely to win again. Its winner takes all, much like in human society. This is known as the Price Principle in the scientific world. Those who have will continue to gain, while those with nothing will continue to receive nothing. Still, even the most powerful can be brought down by two who are ¾ of his strength, so those who wish to stay on top must learn to form reciprocal relationships with those in lower statuses. From the beginning of time, we have had an inborn foundation in our brains about our positions in society. Those with high status expect to keep it; those with low status, even if allowed access to high status, will not know what to do with it. To change this mindset, the best place to start is with the physical. Taking care of yourself at the basic levels, learning to stand tall and look others in the eye, and having a routine is beneficial not just to overall health but the way we perceive ourselves and others. When we stand up straight with our shoulders back, we are signaling to ourselves and others that we are accepting the responsibility of life and willing to face and fight for what is needed.

Rule 2

Rule two is "Treat Yourself like Someone You Are Responsible for Helping." Think of the following example as what applies to rule two. If 100 people are prescribed the same drug, one-third will never fill the prescription for various reasons. On the 67 who fill the prescription, half will not take it correctly by either missing a dose, not finishing it or not taking it. Though pharmacists and physicians blame the patients, psychologists blame the doctors who should have offered advice that would be followed and then ensure it happened correctly. This is in part because psychologists tend to spend much longer with a client than a doctor. Take this a step further, imagine someone who just received an organ transplant after months on a waiting list. The body does not like this and attacks the organ, meaning anti-rejection medications are necessary. Even though a few pills for life are better than a lifetime of something like dialysis, many suffer organ rejection because they do not take these pills. This does not seem to make sense.

This may be because those who require a transplant are likely isolated, depressed, and impaired by other health problems. It could because they could not afford the medication or do not understand the necessity. We may never fully understand. So, think about this in another way, it is not you who is sick, but your dog. You go to the vet, and they offer pills to correct the problem. You care enough to take them to the vet, to get the pills, which shows in your action. In fact, most will care more about that pet than themselves, and this is a problem. Caring for your pet is not an issue; it is a good thing, but you must also learn to care about yourself. There are three aspects to each person's life, some are objective, some subjective, but all exist.

These three areas include chaos, order, and the third is a process that mediates between these extremes. This third is often called consciousness. Our subjugation to chaos and order can make us doubt our existence or importance and fail to care for ourselves.

To clarify, chaos is ignorance and unexplored territory. It is despair we feel when betrayed. It is the situations and things we do not know and understand. By contrast, the order is that which we understand because it has been explored and offers structure. There is a structure in society, and we have adapted based on society, home, religion, and other structures that exist. Order is where the behavior of the world matches both our desires and expectations. This is when things turn out as we expect, but this sometimes turns into tyranny when it is too one-sided. Still, we like to order because it is familiar and we can think of the long-term maintenance. The problem is, every conceivable situation has both chaos and order. There are always things we can control and things we cannot. Meaning is found when we can have order in our lives but have part of our life in chaos as we learn and grow.

Looking back to the first story and question of why people are more likely to give medication to their dogs with regularity than themselves, we go to the very beginning, the Garden of Eden. In the Garden, once the eyes of Adam and Eve were opened, they immediately became self-conscious. This self-consciousness caused them to cover and even hide out of shame. This shame is ingrained in us, and though we may want to care for ourselves, we know our deepest darkest insecurities and issues. This can make us feel unworthy to do something as simple as taking medication. However, when we look at the innocent animal, we see something that is harmless and innocent, therefore deserving. This may seem odd because we know many of our pets are predators. A cat or dog may kill small prey, but we still care for them because this is their nature, and they hold no responsibility for such actions. When we look at ourselves, we must face the morality of our choices and judgment. This can cause us to judge ourselves harshly, even if we may not feel we are being overly judgmental. We feel fallen and not due to the respect of self-care. We are cynical and feel we could never deserve the best care. We must change the way we view ourselves and what is deserved by getting as much out of life as we put into it. This creates strength on both sides of any relationship as both sides are loved, forgiven, and worth the effort needed because it is mutual and equal. Hatefulness and gratefulness must remain balanced. Treating ourselves as we would someone we are responsible for is not what you want or what would make you happy, but what makes you strong and responsible for the future.

Rule 3

Rule three is "Make Friends with People Who Want the Best for You." This chapter starts with a story of the author's hometown—a town of only 3000 people and 400 miles from the nearest town. The idea of cable TV and the internet did not exist for the area, so staying entertained was something that took imagination. This was especially true during the five months of winter when having temperatures of 40 below during the day was the norm and nights were much colder. Hair froze after a shower, and cold air froze eyelashes the moment you walked out the door. The author continues to tell a specific story growing up when he sat in an old car with a friend in winter; the heater had stopped, so as they drove, he had to constantly wipe the window in front of the driver with a vodka-soaked rag so they could see. Stopping was not an option because there was nowhere to stop. The summers left little for children to do, but the winters were even worse with few sunlight hours due to being so far north and very low temperatures. In the winters, friends matter more than anything else because there was little activity.

The story continues about the author's friend, Chris, and his cousin. Chris was smart, loved to read, and was a natural-born engineer. Chris grew up in a good family with soft-spoken parents and sisters who were also smart and otherwise okay, but Chris had missed out on something because he was resentful and angry. This too on a material form in his 1972 blue Ford pickup that was covered in dents all over the body. This included the interior that was dented from passengers being tossed against the different surfaces over time. Each time Chris would wreck his truck, his father would buy him something new, including an ice cream truck and a motorbike at one point. Chris did not ever sell ice cream, nor did he like the bike. Chris did not get along with his father, and they had a poor relationship. Chris's father was diagnosed with an illness after years of problems, and he did not have the energy he should have in dealing with his son; this may have been the totality of the issues.

Chris had a younger cousin, by two years, named Ed. At the age of 12, Ed was witty, smart, and good-looking, but he too drifted downhill. He was never as angry as Chris but was still very confused and barely acknowledged his own existence. Neither boy's situation was improved when they discovered marijuana. Like most other teenagers at that time, the trio spent evenings and weekends just driving around the many roads in the town or, when possible, at a party. The parties were open to most willing to crash, and drinking caused the behavior to quickly become undesirable. Even if parties were not planned, an empty house with lights on and no cars in the driveway meant parents were gone, and the teenager in the house was alone. A party often got started, whether planned or not and went downhill quickly. The author does not look back on these parties nostalgically. It seemed the teens in the town were already cynical, and doing anything that parents tried to organize was rejected.

Those in the town knew by an early age whether they would be staying or leaving. It seemed obvious before the teenage years whether a kid was college-bound or not, and money was not the issue in the small town that was oil-rich and had high paying jobs. In high school, some of the author's friends had already dropped out, and two newcomers were welcomed into the group. These two had come from an even smaller town, but they were amusing, cool, and reliable. One would end up being his roommate in college; the other would attend a different college. Their decision to pursue higher education bolstered the author's as well. The time in school allowed the author to shed much of his past, and while the new chaos was a bit stressful, there were new possibilities as well. While the author attributed this to normal growing up, it was not the same for everyone.

Years later, when the author lived in a city, sharing an apartment with his sister while they both finished college, he heard from Ed. The once bright young man came to visit with a friend, both so stoned that they were barely functioning. Ed worked part-time mowing lawns and doing landscaping, but he walked slow and stooped, obviously unhappy. Chris had not left their small town and, in his 30s, had a psychotic break that had been a long time coming. He committed suicide. It is hard to understand how three people brought up in similar circumstances could end up so differently. The answer is not cut and dry, but when people have a low opinion of themselves or refuse to take personal responsibility, they often choose to stay around others who feel the same way. They do not believe they deserve better, so they never try for better. Some people choose poor friends for another reason, like wanting to rescue them. While it is great and noble to help others, not everyone who is failing is a victim. Victimhood is an easy role to hold because it holds no responsibility.

When we do choose to help someone, we must remember and caution ourselves not to be pulled down by their cynicism. It is much easier for delinquency to spread than stability. Sometimes the most help we can be to a person is to insight them to moving and changing, not forgiving all the failures that have led to the current position. We must also determine why we wish to help. If it is simply to make ourselves look or feel better, it is not genuinely helping. We must also determine before help is offered if the person needs help due to circumstances or has simply settled into their life and has become comfortable in the position. Many people reject an upward path because it is difficult, not because it is not an option. We must choose friends who are good for us, and this can start with a single question about each of your current friends: Would you recommend them to be a friend to your father? Sister? Son? If so, then keep them in your life; if not, it may be time to move on to someone better for your life.

Rule 4

Rule four is "Compare Yourself to Who You Were Yesterday, Not to Who Someone Else is Today." It is easy for people to be good at something in a small town because there are so few people. This may be why people from small towns are overrepresented among those who are eminent. Those from big cities, where most people are from now, may seem like one in a million, but twenty others have the same skill set. Add in technology that connects so many, and that number gets higher and more people are available and great at a single task. No matter how good we may think we are at some task, someone exists that makes us look incompetent in some way. Inside each of us is an internal critic that knows someone else will always be better at some point. This voice is hard to quiet.

The worst part, somewhat ironically, is that this critic is necessary because there are such things as bad art, dangerous food, and tuneless musicians. If these things are not recognized and standards set, then the consequences can be harsh and real. We are not equal in ability or outcome, and it is impossible to ever be such. A small number of people produce a large part of everything, which leaves many on the bottom. No one wants to be at the bottom; it is an unhappy place. Social psychologists recommend "positive illusions" as a way to find mental health, but this is a sad philosophy saying that only delusions can save you from your miserable life. An alternative is to see that the game you are playing is rigged, possibly by yourself, and to stop listening to the critical voice. If that critical voice is critical toward everyone, even if they are great at something, then stop listening to it.

Standards of better or worse are necessary. If something can be done, it can also be done better or worse. To do anything is to play a game with a defined and somehow valued end. Each game comes with either success or failure. If this did not exist, nothing would be worth trying or accomplishing. There is no meaning if there is no difference between better and worse. We must start by considering the words success and failure. The words imply no middle ground, it is either one or the other, but there are always degrees in our complex world. This starts by understanding that there are many games to play that match your individual talents. The world allows for many ways of being, and if one fails, you can try something else. If you cannot seem to succeed at anything, then you can also invent a new game. To expand this, we all play multiple games between career, friends, family, and personal projects. Across the board, you have a spectrum of success and failure. If we find ourselves winning at everything, it may not be that we are truly winning, but not doing anything difficult or new. The winning may continue, but the growth has slowed or stopped. Most of the time, the games we play are so unique to us that it is impossible to compare them to others.

Many of us may overvalue what we do not have available while undervaluing what we are actually doing. Instead, we need to practice gratitude for what is, not what could be. Think of it in this way, a work colleague does better than you on a project, but his wife is having an affair; you have a strong, stable, loving marriage. Who is better off, who is winning? The internal critic chooses one arbitrary domain of comparison and then treats it as the only one relevant. When we are young, we compare ourselves to others because we have no internal standards. As we mature, we are increasingly unique and individual, which makes us less compared to others. We must learn to find what we can do and accomplish and only base our success and failure on our own growth. Once we mature and have our own set of standards, we can no longer logically compare ourselves to others. Others do not have our unique make-up or life, so we must use ourselves and our growth and improvement as the measuring stick. What others do or accomplish is not important for our life; it is only our own life that matters for comparison.

Rule 5

Rule five, "Do Not Let Your Children Do Anything That Makes You Dislike Them," begins with the author observing a three-year-old follow his parents through a crowded airport. Every few seconds, the kid would let out a scream to gain attention for something. His parents should have let him know this was inappropriate, but they were ignoring the screaming child. A few seconds of directed problem solving would have ended the episode that was making others hate the child, but these parents may have just been too tired to worry about it. Another set of parents followed their two-year-old everywhere to micromanage his behavior. This meant he had no real freedom ever, and because he never heard "no," he had no reasonable limits. One final example was experienced by the author's daughter, who was hit by another child with a metal toy truck. The child doing the hitting was picked up by the mother and told not to do that and then comforted in hushed tones. This woman was teaching her child that they could do what they wanted and be comforted, starting the process of making a little God-Emperor that will think they can do no wrong. While there may be some psychological basis to mothers or fathers favoring sons to continue the ancestral line, it can go wrong to create selfish humans.

The author is a clinical psychologist as well and sees clients discuss familial problems. Frequently, the day-to-day issues, though small, are problematic. These are not to be overlooked, though, because the little things are what make up our lives. He spoke with one parent who fought his child to go to bed each night, typically for about 45 minutes. Added up, this was 240 hours a year wasted on fighting with the child just to sleep. Even with the calmest of temperaments, this can lead to a building resentment or at least wasted time that could be spent doing something more enjoyable. Often, parents are blamed for tough children, but this cannot all be laid on parents. Too often, parents fear their children at this time when they are not allowed to discipline and not given credit for conventionality and order. The time in which we live has increased parental sensitivity to short term suffering emotional for their children but heightened the fear of damaging children simultaneously.

Many people still believe that children are a blank slate and only made worse because of parents and society's influence. If this were true, children left alone would develop only positive or good qualities. This is why *Lord of the Flies* was such a popular book. Socialization, understanding the norms of society fosters good and prevents a great deal of harm. Children need to be both shaped and informed, so they can thrive. Children can often suffer as much or more by a lack of incisive attention as physical or mental abuse. Children are damaged when those who are to care for them are afraid to cause conflict or upset and do not offer correction. This leaves children dull and often without friends because they require too much energy and commitment early on. Children tend to befriend others whose cost/benefit ratio is lower.

Parents need to remember that they are not friends with their children. Many modern parents are paralyzed by the fear that their children will not like or love them if they provide discipline in any way. They desire their children's friendship and too often sacrifice respect to earn it. It is important to remember that friends come and go, children will have many, but there are only one set of parents, sometimes just a single parent that must be so much more than a friend. Parents must learn to accept their children's momentary anger toward them to offer corrective action, so children learn about consequences. Parents serve as arbiters of society, and it is their responsibility to discipline their children. Proper discipline requires effort as it is not revenge or anger, but the teaching of consequence for behavior so children can learn, grow, and function in society. Without correction, a child will not undergo the effort filled process or regulating and organizing impulses. They will test boundaries to learn them.

There is a difference between discipline and punishment. They must both be used, and both can be scary, done well or poorly, and applied with a conscious or unconscious manner. Discipline can be accomplished with reward, but it takes planning and practice, a reward given at just the right time. It also takes much more time as the behavior we desire must be observed naturally occurring, not forced, then rewarded. We cannot protect children from all pain and failure in life, but we can help them learn from this pain and failure to the cost/benefit that is worth the failure. If parents do not teach their children the skills necessary in society, society will teach them in harsher ways much later in life. We must teach our children to behave out of love. This requires discipline, reward, and punishment over time. Letting them do things that make us dislike them, even short term means this responsibility is not being taken.

Rule 6

Rule six is stated as "Set Your House in Perfect Order Before You Criticize the World." The chapter starts out recounting the Sandy Hook and Columbine school shootings that had odd religious undertones. These amounted to people who viewed being, specifically human beings, so corrupt and contemptible that they should not exist. The shooters appointed themselves as supreme adjudicators of reality and found it wanting, so sufficiently evil that all should die. The truth is, life is hard, and we will all experience pain and suffering. Sometimes this is due to a personal fault, and we feel people are getting what they deserve, but human control remains limited. The susceptibility to despair, aging, and death is universal, so we are not completely at fault, but who is? Everyone wants someone to blame for an intolerable state, but there is not always a clear cause of an event other than the normal course of life. When people try to help or find a cause, they tend to look at the wrong things. When someone is angry over a situation, we should not ask why they are angry, but how others are not angry. The same is true for drug use; it doesn't matter why people use it, but how others avoid using it. Just because we experience evil does not mean we must perpetuate it. We can learn goodness from experiencing evil.

We need to learn to look at life not as controlled by God or some other being, but by our choices and preparation level. Think of things called natural disasters, like when Katrina flooded New Orleans. Years earlier, the Flood Control Act had mandated that the levee system be updated, but 40 years later, only 60 percent of the work was complete. If the work had been complete, the flood would not have happened to such extreme levels. The hurricane was an act of God, but the failure to prepare was a sin. Suffering is the norm, people are limited in this tragic life, but if suffering becomes unbearable and you are becoming corrupt, then it is time to make some changes. Start by considering your circumstances and figuring out if you have taken full advantage of all opportunities you have been offered. Are you working as hard as possible or holding to bitterness and resentment? Have you made peace with people, and do you treat others with respect? Basically, you need to clean up your life by stopping what you know is wrong. As you learn to do this over months and years, life will improve because it is simpler, and you are stronger. This is setting your house in order before judging the world and others.

Are you enjoying the book so far?

If so, please help us reach more readers by taking 30 seconds to write

just a few words on Amazon.

SCAN ME

Or, you can choose to leave one later...

Rule 7

Rule seven is "Pursue What is Meaningful (Not What is Expedient)." This can be a hard rule to accept, knowing that life is suffering, and an irrefutable truth we must simply accept. Most people, upon this realization, will pursue pleasure by following impulses to live for the moment. This can lead to lying, stealing, and manipulating because the universe is meaningless. This is how many people justify living in such a manner, focusing on selfish, immediate gratification. However, even early on, in biblical times, our forefathers engaged in sacrifice to please God. Many years ago, they started learning that sacrificing something of value now may lead to something better in the future. The sacrifice of now is to gain benefit later. This is why we work and possibly why a sacrifice was discussed in the Bible so soon after the Fall. Sacrifice and work are uniquely human. Animals may appear to work at times, but they are just following a dictate of nature.

So, we can know that sacrifice leads to future gains and assume that larger sacrifices lead to larger gains. Sacrifice improves the future, but this must be fleshed out for better understanding. It is hard to work against our ancestral nature that demands immediate satisfaction. This likely developed out of conditions of deprivation. Still, the realization that pleasure could be forestalled is one we accept with difficulty. This is because it requires a stabilized civilization to delay gratification. This is partly because if the future is uncertain or the things you sacrificed will disappear, then immediate gratification is necessary. Since society is largely stabilized, at least as far as basic necessities, delayed gratification is possible. This can lead to sharing because there tends to be excess. When we share, we initiate a process of trade, even if it is not at that moment, but for the future. If a child is willing to share their toys, others will be more likely to be their friends and share with them. Benjamin Franklin said that if someone new came into a neighborhood, they should ask neighbors to do something small. This is an invitation to social interaction and creates a first encounter. It also opened the person being asked up to favor in the future, increasing familiarity.

It is better to have something over nothing, but even better to share generously because that is lasting and reliable. If the world seems against us, then it may be time to examine our values because we see the world through our values. We must let go of presuppositions and possibly sacrifice what we love best, so we can gain in the long run. It requires sacrifice to become who we might be instead of who we are while holding on to the same old things. This is illustrated in the old tale about catching a monkey. It is said to catch a monkey; you should find a jar with a narrow opening just large enough for a monkey to reach in. Then, fill the bottom with stones to weigh it down and scatter a few treats in the jar that monkeys enjoy. Scatter a few more treats around to draw the monkey. When it comes, it will reach in to grab the treats and not be able to take its paw free without losing the treats. The monkey will not do this even if it means sacrificing itself to capture. Freedom would be as easy as letting go, but they are unwilling. Humans often behave in the same way. We are unwilling to let go of something precious, even if something better is possible. If instead, we learn to live properly and fully, then we can discover meaning in our life to the point that we do not even fear death.

Humans are self-conscious beings, and this produces inevitable suffering. This suffering then motivates selfish gratification to eliminate short term suffering. If we can suffer mildly short term by offering sacrifice, then long term suffering may be alleviated. This is an issue in and of itself, but the evil compounds the problem in society. When Adam and Eve ate the fruit, they were immediately aware of good and evil. This knowledge is a curse because we now know how to feel pain and fear and cause others to feel it. This is seen in Cain and Abel. Abel and Cain both sacrificed to God, but only Abel's was accepted. We do not know why, but it is assumed because Cain's heart was not right with God. Cain would have immediately been jealous because he had tried and done what was appropriate in his mind but failed for no reason. A lack of reason made Cain jealous and rebellious. He confronted God, accused Him, and cursed creation. God responds that the fault is with Cain and his sin; this was just the consequences of his actions. To Cain, this was insult added to injury. Cain knows how to cause pain and does so by killing his brother. Cain turned to evil to get what he wanted. The point is we have a choice. It is ours to make in light of human nature and society. We may not get all we want or desire immediately, but the sacrifice will be worth it long term.

Rule 8

Rule eight is written as "Tell the Truth – Or at Least, Don't Lie." This sounds like the same thing, but it will be further explained. Once again, beginning with a story, the author describes an interaction at a hospital that still had a few permanent psych patients. He was with a group of other first-year students waiting for the professor when a small, frail woman walked up to the waiting group, asked what they were doing, and asked if she could join. This was asked to another female student that was standing beside the author. The easy answer that would have saved face would have been a white lie. Something like, oh, we are just leaving or something along those lines. This would have kept future doctors and long-term patients on equal ground, but his conscience would not allow such a lie. The author answered for the other students and said we are training as doctors, and she could not join. The woman was hurt, but only for a moment, and then went on her way. This was just the culmination of what the author had learned about himself a few years prior. In realizing what compulsions he often had but never acted on, he started to look at his own life. He realized that most of what he spoke was untrue, though there were motives like winning an argument, looking intelligent, or meeting people that backed these untruths. He used language to twist the world into delivering what he felt was needed.

In realizing how fake he was being, the author chose to start telling the truth, saying only what the internal voice did not object to, but he would not lie when this was not possible. Telling the truth is what we should do when we do not know what to do. This came in handy a few years later when dealing with a paranoid patient. The patient was paranoid, not stupid, but shared his vivid, horrible fantasies with the author. The author told him when he understood how the fantasies made him feel, and even when he was mad. The patient trusted the author because he was honest, even if that honesty was rarely to the positive. Around the same time, the author and his wife had a landlord that they lived next door to and his girlfriend, who had the marks of a self-injurer. The girlfriend soon killed herself, and the landlord, an ex-biker gang leader, turned to alcohol, which he had been trying to quit. On occasion, the landlord would show up in the middle of the night trying to sell some item to his tenants, and on occasion, the author would buy them, knowing it was to feed his alcohol habit. This upset the author's wife, who liked the landlord but did not think they should help a habit he was trying to stop.

The author decided he would tell the man the truth when he showed up again, and it did not take long. At two in the morning, the landlord showed up very drunk, trying to sell his toaster for money to get booze. The author calmly told him that he knew he was trying to quit drinking and that providing him with more money would not be good for him. He said that the act made his wife nervous. This was met with a long, silent gaze, but the landlord left and never approached them again to sell anything. He was not angry but took the truth to heart, and it built their relationship on a stronger foundation. Telling the truth is a much different pathway than telling half-truths and white lies. Words can be used to manipulate the world, known as being politically correct, but just spin. A life lived in this way is based on two premises. The first is that current knowledge is enough to define well and that reality would be unbearable if left to its own. The first premise is unjustifiable, but the second is worse. This is pride and arrogance to some degree, feeling that all we know is all that needs to be known. People who live this way create ideals and Eden's of the mind and then bend their lives to attempt to make it happen with little forethought. These same people will be loathed to admit that the initial goal may be wrong because this figuratively opens Pandora's Box.

On the other hand, if we are willing to boldly confront the unknown, we can build a renewed self and form new thoughts and goals. Scientifically speaking, new genes have been discovered that turn on when we are in novel situations. These genes code for new proteins in the body and form new structures in the brain. If we never experience anything new, these parts of the brain will remain in stasis. Put another way, whatever we do or do not do affects us overall. We can keep trying new things and situations to grow or remain incomplete. Either way, it affects our character. It is important to remember that reality will never be improved through falsehoods. When we learn to accept the truth, it requires sacrifice. This is not easy, but it is for the best. We need to work toward our authentic selves, which is what happens when we try something and then look at the results. If what we wanted do not happen, then our method or aim was wrong, and we need to learn more. Those living inauthentically in the same situation will not learn, but grow jealous, blame others, and see the world as unfair. We must learn not just to tell the truth to others, but ourselves as well. Life is about suffering, but how we handle that truth makes a huge difference.

Rule 9

Rule nine, "Assume That the Person You are Listening to Might Know Something You Don't," starts with saying that psychotherapy is not advice. Psychotherapy is a conversation when advice is what people give when they want to demonstrate their intelligence or simply get you to stop talking. Genuine conversation is about exploring, strategizing, and articulating as you speak, but mostly listen. Listening, truly listening, helps you learn about people, what they want, their problems, and how they plan to fix them. Sometimes, you may even hear things that help you fix an issue in your own life. Therapy offers people a chance to talk and to listen. They may need someone to talk to or need to listen as someone else speaks. Either way, things are often revealed or brought into a new light as information or feelings are shared. The author speaks of one patient who shared with him during several sessions.

The patient was a well-dressed businesswoman by all appearances, but she had never really had a real job and was extremely lonely. One day she came in and randomly and unexpectedly announced she "thought" she had been raped several times. She explained the situation about going to a bar on different nights, meeting someone, and ending up in bed only to awake the next morning, unsure of motives or what had happened. As she discussed, she remembered what she could, but we must always be aware that the present can change the past and the future the present because of the new lens we are viewing it through. As we remember the past, we have memories of some things but not others, even though the memories may hold equal importance. We categorize our memories and experiences, often in seemingly arbitrary ways. Our memories are also subjective because we each have vested interests in different things, pay attention to different aspects of life.

As for the patient, the author had a few choices; he could tell the patient that she was potentially raped unless she gave consent at every move. He could have told her she was a perpetual victim that was reliving and punishing men due to past abuse. He could have told her she was behaving in a way that led her down the victim's pathway. Instead, he listened and just let her talk. Talking allows people to think, and people need this. Thinking is an internal dialogue between differing worldviews that we are arguing with ourselves. This helps us conclude and decision, then move on in our lives, sometimes with changed views. Many times, a therapist is the other half of this conversation, not to answer questions or offer an opinion, but to listen as the person speaks. This is healthy and helpful. A good therapist will be a good listener and simply allow their patients to talk, even if it does not make sense at first. This keeps patients from taking in the opinions of their therapist and therapist from taking on the problems of their patients. However, some people want a closer relationship with therapists, so a conversation is important, not something one-sided and disconnected. This has its own dangers but is also possible.

We have to get along with other people, and a therapist is one of those people. A good therapist will tell you the truth of what they think about what is said or done, offering at least one honest opinion about what is shared. Whether a therapist or not, listening is important and dangerous because it is transformative. To learn to be a good listener, try the following. Feel free to speak up for yourself and offer an opinion only after restating what the other person has said. This can be helpful and often changes the listener as they restate what is said. This type of listening also aids the person in the utility of memory. Repeating something moves it deeper into your memory. By learning to listen, we can learn about ourselves and others. True listening is never boring and always full of information if we are willing to do it correctly.

Rule 10

Rule ten for life is "Be Precise in Your Speech." Though the initial story seems unrelated at first, it is worth sharing. Most of us have a computer or laptop. We see the black or grey box, see the keyboard, and know the mouse moves the cursor. Still, most of what we see is not really the computer, the information center; it is the shell. That part we do not see will also be completely obsolete in five years. This is because even though the laptop is impressive and expensive now, it is one note in a symphony that is played by millions. It is a minuscule part of something much larger that is forgotten as the symphony moves forward. Thinking of it in another way, the computer is a single leaf in a giant forest. You may touch or pluck off a branch that can be seen as a single entity briefly, but this tends to lead to a misconception of the forest, not a clarification. Without its attachment to the tree, the leaf will wither, die, and disappear, just as a computer does not function long without an operating system or electricity. So much of what are laptops do is actually outside the reaches of their boxed boundaries, which is why they are only important for a few years before becoming outdated. Almost all we see is like this, but we often do not notice.

When we look at the world, we see things, or at least we think we do so we can categorize them in our brains. We tend to look at objects as useful or in the way, so we do not see objects; we are attributing meaning. When we see a floor, we see something to walk on, a door, something to open and walkthrough. A beanbag chair and stump fall into the same category because both can serve as a seat. We see tools and obstacles, not things and objects. We further categorize these tools into categories of usefulness or danger based on our abilities and needs. We even see people's faces because we need to communicate and work with them, but we do not see the cells or subcellular atoms that create the face we view. We also do not see the larger picture of their social circle, their activities, or them across the expanse of time. We perceive things and even people in their sufficiency for our purpose. For this reason, we must be precise in our aim, or we will be overwhelmed by all the complexity of the world. This holds true even for self-perceptions.

We perceive that we end at our skin, but if we are willing, we can understand that we shift what is inside our skin based on the context we inhabit. When we do something simple like picking up a screwdriver, our body adjusts to include an appendage holding the tool. When we stretch our arms, we automatically adjust to the added length. Looked at another way, we become possessive of the tool. Think of driving a car, just another tool, but an angry person bangs on the hood, and we take it personally. It is not us, but we perceive it to be. The extensible boundaries that we have of ourselves can include other people as well. A mother is usually willing to sacrifice herself for her children. We must ask ourselves which sacrifice we would rather make, an arm, a leg, a child, a husband. We practice extending ourselves experimentally before specifying which path to take. This happens on a larger scale as well. Think of a sports game in which thousands of fans seem to rise to their feet simultaneously when their team makes a goal. It is like everyone is connected and responds in an instant. Fans all become one at that moment. This coming together makes cooperation easy because we rely on the same innate mechanisms that drive us to protect our bodies.

It can be difficult to sense the connected chaos that is reality if we are just looking at it. The boundaries between the different levels of things are not clear or objective but established pragmatically. However, they retain this validity only under narrow conditions when things go according to our plan. Think of our systems like a car. We do not often think about our car when it is working, but if something happens and it no longer starts or moves, we realize that we have little knowledge of the smaller parts. We may go to a mechanic but then worry whether they are trustworthy or competent. We may worry we are driving on horrible roads or concerned that we made a poor vehicle choice, even though this was never a concern when the car was running.

When things break in some way, we are faced with what we have been ignoring. These problems were always lurking below, but we chose not to see or notice because they were not yet problems. When this happens, we tend to react before thinking. Ancient reflexes take over to protect us. If we ignore the chaos, never confront it, it rises and engulfs us. If we face it, go through it, and learn, we become stronger. We must face it precisely, though, in such a way that we know what we are facing, just as pain can be anything unless we are specific about it with our doctor and find the exact cause. Even if the diagnosis ends up tragic, it is at least specific. This allows us a path to take, specific knowledge of what is, not what could be.

Rule 11

Rule eleven is "Do Not Bother Children When They are Skateboarding.: This one seems a bit obvious because we should not distract anyone when they are taking part in something that could lead to injury, but there is a deeper implication in this rule. This chapter opens with a story of the author watching skateboarders, often boys, at his place of business. The area had a set of concrete stairs and a wide rounded banister down the center. The skateboarders would push back, gather speed, and board down the railing, hopefully on their board, but some were not so lucky. Whether successful or not, they were soon back to it. It was impressive and dangerous, but the danger was the point. They were trying to be triumphant over this danger by becoming competent in the skill. Just around the corner on a different street were concrete planter boxes that the skateboarders used to boardslide down, but then little metal brackets appeared called skate stoppers, and this trick ended. Unfortunately, the skate stoppers also gave the design of the garden boxes and sculpture a prison-like appearance when it was supposed to bring beauty to the area. Seeing this happen reminded the author of a story he had just read.

The story was that two weeks before an elementary school starting, all playground equipment was removed because of panic over insurability. The playgrounds were safe and grandfathered in for insurability, which was often paid for by parents. However, this meant no playgrounds for over a year. Kids found stuff to do, often being on the roof of the local school or playing in the dirt because they were bored. The playground had been sufficiently safe, which is the term used because if they are too safe, kids quit playing or find unintended ways to play. Kids, all people, need things to remain challenging, a bit dangerous, to stay interested. This allows for continued development. If things are made too safe, people find ways to make them dangerous again. We are hard-wired to enjoy risk, though some at lower levels than others, and get excited about optimizing future performance. When overprotected, we will fail when something inevitable and dangerous comes into our lives.

Looking into depth psychologists, we see that everything has a dark side. We can choose to acknowledge the dark side, confront it, or fall into it allowing ourselves to be overwhelmed. The dark side of things that engulfs people are those who seem to hate humans, likely even themselves, to such a degree that they think humans should be destroyed. This can lead to a very dark and scary life. This does not mean the dark side should be ignored because it does exist, and we need to make the best of what we have to survive and thrive. Think of this in terms of gender, a current hot button issue. People argue for gender equality, but genders are actually more well defined when gender equality is pushed, like in many Scandinavian countries. In countries which gender equality is the norm when children enter puberty, the girls tend to pull toward people and the boys toward things and interests. In all countries, boys and girls are treated differently. A boy is a winner when they excel among their male peers in "boy" type activities, but girls are considered a success when they participate and win in either boy or girl activities. This continues at the university levels, where the population is predominantly female. In 15 years, if trends continue, few men at universities will not be good news for men or women.

Men will end up in low paying jobs, which will cause women, who tend to marry across or up to have fewer options. This leaves men in low paying positions, and women largely unprotected financially if they choose to have children. While the patriarchy may be oppressive, all culture is oppressive by structure. However, when we think about culture only as oppressive, it is ungrateful and ignorant, and highly dangerous. This does not mean that culture should not be criticized at times, but that it should be criticized, knowing that changes will bring both victories and losses over time. To have absolute equality, we sacrifice the value of all things as well. This would leave us with nothing to live for because nothing mattered. Even if we can easily buy into the patriarchy, it was not men alone who created culture. Even if we could assume only men ever made art, decisions, and laws, it requires women to birth, raise, and allow these men to exist. Culture is not predominantly male or female; it takes both to exist. Women and men have struggled against similar challenges, though women often faced harder times overall. Still, all have grown and changed. Men have not only helped men, and women have not only helped women in our culture, so why teach children that our culture is only full of male oppression. It is dangerous to believe that categorization is only about exclusion, as power plays an obvious part, as do many other things. People who become resentful over things are either being taken advantage of or refuse to take responsibility and grow up for life. We must take moral responsibility for ourselves first and then work to change policies and beliefs that are unfair. However, any change comes with good and bad, which cannot always be predicted. Based on the first story, the skateboarders were stopped, but the beauty of the garden structures was ruined, its purpose now pointless.

Rule 12

Rule twelve, the final rule, is "Pet a Cat When You Encounter One on the Street." Though this seems like a silly rule, it is flanked by a disclaimer that dogs are okay too. The author owns a dog bought for his daughter. The American Eskimo dog was not his daughter's first animal, but it was their first dog due to allergies. She had been allergic to typical pets, but the American Eskimo was hypoallergenic. The animal's small face and awkward movements as a puppy were endearing and called out the caretaker in all around. The dog is highly intelligent and learns new skills well, though it is hard to tell if he truly enjoys them. He has many nicknames and even his own hashtag. The author admits he is describing his dog to avoid running afoul of a phenomenon called "minimal group identification," as discovered by Henri Tajfel, a psychologist. His research started by bringing people into a room to show them a screen with dots and asking them to estimate the number. The people were then put in groups as accurate or inaccurate, over or under estimators. Then he gave them money to divide among the groups. This showed that subjects displayed a preference for those in their own group, rejecting egalitarian distribution and rewarding those they identified within the moment. This showed two more things; people are both social and antisocial. People are social because they identify with members of their own group, but antisocial because they don't like members of a different group. This is true, no matter how arbitrarily the groups have been assigned.

When two or more factors are important, but one cannot be maximized without limiting or diminishing the other, a problem arises. The problem is that there is antipathy between cooperation and competition, but both are needed. Cooperation is for safety, and competition is for status and personal growth. Both are psychologically desirable. If a group is too small, it does not have enough power and prestige to fend off other groups, but one too large makes it too difficult to reach the top. People want to organize and protect themselves and want a probability of climbing to the top of a given group. This is in part why a dog story started this chapter that was a rule about cats so that no one would feel left out.

The idea that life is suffering is true of every religious doctrine because humans are fragile. This can be hard to accept, and we may wonder why anyone hopes to thrive or even exist under such conditions. Still, if we think this through, we realize that what makes a person we love and appreciate is inseparable from their limitations. This is mostly realized with a sick child. A small and sick child may seem unfair, but if we could fix every pain, correct every aspect of their being so they could never be hurt again, they would no longer be themselves. Without our limitations, we do not exist. They are linked. If we believe life includes suffering, we can get bogged down in the abyss, especially if that is all we think about. We have the alternative of ignoring suffering completely, but this only numbs to reality. Instead, we must find some balance, knowing suffering exists, but that it is also necessary to exist. We must learn to notice things. We love someone because of their limitations, not despite them. We learn to notice yet accept. This does not mean we should stop trying to make life better, but we must do so within limits, so humanity itself does not disappear.

Dogs are like people. They are hierarchical, social, and domesticated, happy to be at the bottom of the family pyramid. They repay the attention we give with admiration, love, and loyalty. They are wonderful creatures.

Cats are their own creatures and are neither social nor hierarchical, with the only semi-domestication. They choose when to be friendly on their terms and tend to refuse tricks. Dogs are trainable, but cats make decisions. Cats choose to interact with us based on their decisions. They are a manifestation of nature in an almost pure form. When you are walking down the street, you may see a cat. Sometimes, if you call them, sometimes of their own accord, they will come to you. At times, they ignore you or run away. On those times when they come over and allow you to pet them, it can be a bright spot on a dark day or a sunnier spot on a bright day. We need to find points in our day to look for bright spots. Whether it's a cat who graces you with its presence, a child dancing on the street because they just left ballet class, or a hobby that distracts you from pain for a few happy moments, this is how the wonder of being, of existing, makes up for the suffering of that same existence.

Background Information about
12 Rules for Life: An Antidote to Chaos

1 2 Rules for Life: An Antidote to Chaos was written based on a post that was created by the author in response to an online questionnaire. The list received many upvotes and gained popularity, which was the basis of this book. The 12 rules were refined and organized into this book that offers people a way to make sense of the chaos and suffering in life. Life is not easy, fair, or always predictable, but this does not mean we should give up or do away with the human race. We will not find a solution in which all things are fair because if we do, all things simultaneously lose value. The book is not meant to focus readers on the negative things of life, though they do exist and should be noticed, to help change the focus to those things we can control, change, and survive, finding joy along the way.

Background Information about
Jordan B. Peterson

Jordan Peterson is a Canadian clinical psychologist and a psychology professor at the University of Toronto. He first started receiving widespread attention for his political and cultural views in 2010 and has since created a few books, taught classes, and released a series of YouTube videos. Peterson is a family man with a wife and two children that support his work and studies in human nature, politics, and general culture. Inspired by his studies and his childhood, Peterson wrote *12 Rules for Life* that has become a bestseller in several countries. Peterson put both his clinical practice as a psychologist and his teaching duties on hold in 2018 to publish this book and do a world tour.

Trivia Questions

1) How should you stand to help yourself appear stronger and more competent?.

2) What is the general rule about choosing friends?

3) What animal, introduced in the beginning, is highly territorial and will fight for what it wants and needs?

4) What are two ways in which cats and dogs differ according to the book?

5) Which songbird is small but violent and territorial, according to the book?

6) Approximately how many people out of 100, when given a prescription, will use it correctly?

7) What happened to Chris from the author's hometown?

8) What did Chris's truck represent with all its dents and dings?

9) Why is it important for parents to set limits?

10) Why is it useless to remove playground equipment or make it safe?

Discussion Questions

1) Is it truly bad for children to be friends with their parents? Explain your answer.

2) Do you think people are more likely to care for others over themselves, especially those who are suffering? Explain your answer.

3) Have you had friends that have brought you down in life or those that have helped you improve? What happened to each set?

4) Why is it better to compare ourselves to ourselves rather than others? Explain.

5) Do you feel delayed gratification is worth the sacrifice? Explain your answer.

6) What deeper meaning can be gained from the differences shared about cats and dogs? Explain your answer.

7) Do you think religion or religious beliefs are at fault for the school shootings mentioned? Explain.

8) Do you think it is best to always tell the truth? Explain your answer.

9) Is suffering a normal part of life that should be accepted without question? Explain your answer.

10) Is true equality across all areas truly possible? Explain your thoughts.

Thank You!

Hope you've enjoyed your reading experience.

We here at Book Tigers will always strive to deliver to you the highest quality guides.

So I'd like to thank you for supporting us and reading until the very end.

Before you go, would you mind leaving us a review on Amazon?

It will mean a lot to us and support us in creating high-quality guides for you in the future.

Thanks once again and here's where you can leave a review:

SCAN ME

Warmly yours,

The Book Tigers Team

Download Your Free Gift

Before you go any further, why not pick up a gift from us to you?

Investing In You – Using the Power of Positive Thinking.

You will understand the true power of your positive thinking and subconscious mind and you will have absolute control over them, very fast!

Scan the QR code to get it before it expires!

Discover the Book Tigers Series

If you are enjoying reading our books, please take a moment and check our book series.

SELF HELP & SUCCES SUMMARIES

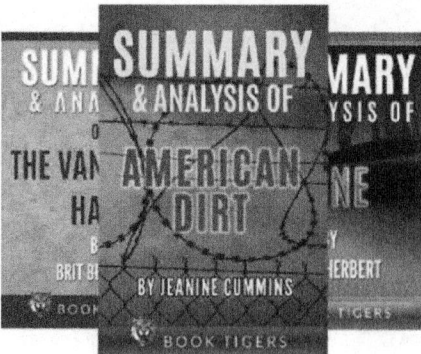

FICTION SUMMARIES

SOCIAL & POLITICS SUMMARIES

HEALTH & DIET SUMMARIES

Feel free to continue your journey with us, where you will find new resources, tools, blogs, and advance notice of new books at...

www.booksandsummaries.com

SCAN ME

Printed in Great Britain
by Amazon